OPEN LETTERS TO AMERICA

OPEN LETTERS TO AMERICA

★★★ **KEVIN POWELL** ★★★

SOFT SKULL PRESS

NEW YORK

KEVIN POWELL

OPEN LETTERS TO AMERICA

Library of Congress Cataloging-in-Publication Data is available.

ISBN: 978-1-59376-214-8

Cover and interior design by Kerry DeBruce of KLAD Creative
Printed in the United States of America

Soft Skull Press
An Imprint of COUNTERPOINT
2117 Fourth Street
Suite D
Berkeley, CA 94710

www.softskull.com
www.counterpointpress.com

Distributed by Publishers Group West

10 9 8 7 6 5 4 3 2 1

For Gloria Steinem and Susan Taylor—open, free,
and true reflections of the limitless possibilities of the human spirit

"If civilization is to survive,

we must cultivate the science of human

relationships — the ability of all peoples, of all kinds,

to live together, in the same world at peace."

—*Franklin D. Roosevelt*

★ ★ ★ ★ ★ ★

"Nobody's free until everybody's free."

—*Fannie Lou Hamer*

★★★ TABLE OF CONTENTS ★★★

OPEN LETTERS TO AMERICA

OPEN LETTER TO
Young America

Saturday, April 4, 2009

Dear Young America:

I've started and stopped this letter to you several times before. The magnitude of these times has been both my muse and my chief distraction. All these months since you, we, elected Barack Obama president of the United States, I have yet to rejoice the way many of you have. There has been great pride, no question, and a sense of relief at this new chapter in American history. But beneath my pride and

> I NEVER THOUGHT I WOULD LIVE TO WITNESS SOMEONE WHO LOOKED LIKE ME BECOMING PRESIDENT.

sense of relief are both an element of shock and, for sure, anxiety. Shock in the sense that I never thought I would live to witness someone who looked like me becoming president. And certainly not someone with the name of Barack Hussein Obama. And shock, too, because, like me, President Obama is the product of a single mother, an absent father, an extended family, and so much movement in his early life that he did not fully grasp the significance of his own name, his own identity, until many years later. So I view Barack Obama as an ordinary American—we are all ordinary Americans—who accomplished something extraordinary on this Earth because he had the audacity to believe in himself and the possibilities of the hard-to-obtain American dream. Dream Mr. Obama did, and the anxiety reached a boiling point for me as I watched the millions of Americans descend on Washington, D.C., for the inauguration. I, too, planned to be there, but when the University of Dayton called me to deliver a Dr. King holiday lecture on the same day Mr. Obama was to place his hand on that inaugural Bible, I chose the Midwest instead. It's as if I wanted a safe emotional distance from it all: the media hype, the sensationalized merchandise, the overpriced parties, the shameless efforts of some to feign connections to the Obamas' inner circle. We in America had never seen anything like this, and we had the inalienable right to bask in the glow of what we'd accomplished, together. But I could not write a single word about it because not only was I baffled by the spectacle of it all, I was also in the midst of a very lengthy period of mourning and, to be mad candid, depression. I was coming to terms with losing a congressional race here in Brooklyn, New York, and with the character assassination and divisiveness dredged up during the campaign. I expected resistance from some corners, but the degree of ugliness and hate levied toward me took a toll on my mental state.

Just as the election ended on Tuesday, September 9, 2008, I received word from my mother that her sister, my oldest aunt, had died of kidney failure due to diabetes complications. I cried shamelessly at my aunt's funeral. In the period that followed, I had moments of deep sadness and displacement, trying to figure out what America means to me, now, in the aftermath of Barack Obama's victory, my campaign loss, and my aunt's lonely and terrible last few days of life. In a word I had been trying to heal . . .

But what finally got me on my way and out of my slump was you, young America. You in Dayton, Ohio, drenched in tears of euphoria on that bitterly cold January day. You in Virginia who stated, without wavering one bit, that you too could be president one day. You in South Carolina, my family's home state, who suddenly and forthrightly walked with your head higher, a sweeping gait of promise and a brand new swagger. You in Kansas, self-assured now that your vote finally counted. And you here in my beloved Brooklyn, who still wear your Obama hats, t-shirts, and buttons these many months since the historic night of November 4, 2008, as if the magic of those trinkets will somehow penetrate your being and transform you into an iconic beacon of change and hope.

And I am writing to you, to us, really, two generations: X and Y born between the mid-1960s and about 1990. We have arrived at an incredible time in American history, a time where words like "activist" and "organizer" have become fashionable again, a time where so many of us are rethinking our life purposes and goals. For the first time in nearly two decades, we are making a commitment to help others. I could not have imagined this twenty-five years ago as a wild-eyed, eighteen-year-old freshman on the campus of Rutgers University in New Brunswick, New Jersey.

It was the era of Ronald Reagan and the Reagan Revolution, and I was just grasping what that would mean for me and for America. Young Republicans were everywhere, and what was particularly striking to me was not only that they had a dynamic, charismatic leader in Reagan, but also that they had something even more powerful: a holistic plan of action. Republicans took over the White House and created an army of young followers dedicated for the long haul. They elected up-and-coming Republicans to congressional, state, and local positions; they propelled conservative media personalities like Rush Limbaugh to shape the dialogue on everything American; and they redirected our religious and spiritual conversations with powerhouse organizations like the Christian Coalition. Like the Obama juggernaut, the Reagan Revolution was also about "change." I did not agree with the change that movement generated, but I could not deny the power of it, just as we cannot deny the power, today, of what President Obama's victory has stirred in our restless souls.

As impressive as the Reagan Revolution was, it was the presidential candidacy of the Reverend Jesse Jackson in 1984 and 1988 that truly captured my youthful imagination and energies. In some ways, he embodied the very factors that would later propel Barack Obama onto the national stage. Jackson was also a fired-up, forty-something candidate who spoke of a "hope" that ordinary people could be agents for the common good. He preached of bringing America together. His campaign for the people was fueled by his magnetism: Here was a Southern preacher with a Civil Rights pedigree and none other than Dr. Martin Luther King Jr. for an early mentor. Handsome and articulate, Jackson could bring people to tears. Regardless of what some of us may think of Rev. Jackson these days (and I certainly have criticisms of his leadership and vision since that time), his campaigns transformed my mind and my life just as a generation later Barack Obama has transformed the minds and lives of today's young Americans. Jackson's 1984 presidential bid in particular is the single reason why I became a political science major at Rutgers, why I became a student leader, and why I decided, then and there at all of eighteen, to dedicate my life to public service.

THERE IS NO DENYING NOW THAT MY MOTHER WAS THE VERY FIRST LEADER, THE VERY FIRST ACTIVIST, THE VERY FIRST ORGANIZER I EVER MET. You see, I had been incredibly shy and awkward growing up. My voice came out in barely decipherable bursts: quick-speak born in urban America and remixed with the South Carolina Geechee accent of my mother's roots. Truth be told, I was terrified that what I had to say would matter to no one including myself—my youthful self-esteem was that low at times. When I first heard Rev. Jackson say "I am somebody," it was as if someone had thrown a piano out a window, onto my unsuspecting head. Until that moment, I knew that I was a human being, a young man, Black—that I was some*thing*. But to be told, as if he were speaking directly to me, that I was some*body*, it was akin to lifting a veil, unloosening the chains, opening a door I had not known even existed. For the very first time, I felt that my thoughts and my voice mattered. When I think back on it now, my becoming an activist, an organizer, and what I guess some would call a leader, was inevitable. I come from a single mother with a grade school education, extreme poverty, fatherlessness, violence all about me, large pockets of despair, and, yes, a profound sense of alienation. In spite of those circumstances, my young mother used her voice to demand a better public school education for me, her only child. She was equally adamant about quality housing and the basic services that can make or break a mother, a son, a family, a life, our lives.

I didn't realize it until much later, but there is no denying now that my mother was the very first leader, the very first activist, the very first organizer I ever met. She knew that if she did not muster the nerve, she and I would be doomed to an existence where "change" would never occur. So it was only a matter of time before I followed in her footsteps. How I would do so still shocks me to this day. You see, it is no small leap to transform oneself from a blindly patriotic young person enrolled in ROTC to a mouthpiece that roared at every instance of inequality, discrimination, or oppression—real or imagined. One moment I was timid and invisible, the next brazen and outspoken. It was both thrilling and liberating.

I participated in the Anti-Apartheid Movement that exploded on college campuses across the globe. I had never heard of South Africa, apartheid, Nelson and Winnie Mandela, the African National Congress, the Pan-African Congress, or Steve Biko until my eyes were opened by this worldwide cause. I did voter education work in the American North and helped disenfranchised voters reregister in the American South. I marched against racial hate crimes across New York City in places like Howard Beach, Queens, and Bensonhurst, Brooklyn. I worked in New York City's infamous welfare hotels and cofounded a North Carolina summer camp for welfare youth. Between the ages of eighteen and twenty-four, I participated in every kind of organization imaginable. In the process I began to see myself as a drum major for justice. But along the way I made many costly mistakes: I was too angry, too often. I had a low tolerance for those who did not share my views. I did not respect women leaders

IT WAS MANY YEARS BEFORE I REALIZED THAT ACTIVISM MUST BE ROOTED IN THE VERY SIMPLE PRINCIPLE OF LOVE.

because I had yet to develop the emotional and political maturity to comprehend the power of sexism amongst us. I did not understand the importance of coalition building with people who were different from me. I sacrificed my grades, my relationships, my emotional and spiritual development, and, yes, my sanity, all for one political agenda or another. Reactive rage was my dominant form of social expression, when it should have been proactive passion and loads of patience. It was many years before I realized that activism must be rooted in the very simple principle of love: love of some kind of moral or spiritual guidepost (some call their guidepost "God"), love of self, love for each other, and, unquestionably, love for humankind. Because I did not base my work on that foundation of love, I failed to reach beyond the battles that were convenient for me. I opposed racism, but injustices like sexism, classism, homophobia, and religious intolerance should also have been on my agenda. It took me years to understand that all the leadership, public service, and community work cannot mask our inadequacies as human beings. We must work on ourselves as we work for the people.

And so it was for me that well into my twenties I fought and protested and screamed and cursed and cried. I really believed, deep in the base of my soul, that no matter how misguided I might have been, my work was a blow for freedom, a blow against injustice. But something happened along the way, young America: One by one those of us who had been filled with baby-faced idealism grew profoundly tired. Our wild eyes were now bloodshot or a dull gray; our laughs of joy now punctuated by tinges of cynicism; and the boundless quest for change now tempered by the harsh realities of life, work, family responsibilities, and the uneasy realization that change is a road seldom traveled by the multitudes.

For the next decade, I set aside my public service work and instead focused on my writing career. In the early 1990s, I grew deeply involved in the spoken word scene. In 1992, by sheer accident, I wound up on the very first season of the now pioneering reality television show MTV's *The Real World*. Then in 1993, I became a founding staff member of Quincy Jones's *Vibe* magazine, the fastest-growing pop-culture publication in American history. Between my experiences with MTV and *Vibe*, I saw firsthand the power of the media and pop culture to both reach young America and speak on its behalf. I had no political agenda whatsoever when I was selected to be on *The Real World*; it did not occur to me at that young age how powerfully my words and actions would affect young people across America. But, my God, did they. This was the very first show of its kind. We weren't performing for the cameras to enhance our "fame" or "careers." What you saw is who we were, raw and unfiltered. For me that meant young America saw me as I was in 1992: a struggling writer doing poetry readings at Manhattan's Nuyorican Poets Café and teaching high school and college writing classes; a mentor to a troubled young man from Brooklyn named Morris; and someone who was quick to passionately challenge my roommates around racism. Add to that how I wore my hair at the time—the immensely popular high-top fade of the day, uncombed and purposely uncontrollable—and the power of popular culture brought my Rutgers brand of politics into living rooms nationwide. It was mind-boggling, to say the least. When we cast members were flown to Los Angeles for MTV's annual Video Music Awards, young people screamed our names as if we were the Beatles. Even more surreal was being recognized on the streets of New York City by folks who would literally chase me requesting autographs, opportunities to talk, and more. While I did not necessarily appreciate the "angry Black male" moniker that stuck with me for years, I could not imagine how greatly that first season would impact so many young Americans.

Equally powerful was the wide-reaching influence of the newly launched *Vibe* magazine. It was there that I would become the primary journalist in the country to interview the late Tupac Shakur during his short twenty-five-year life. In 1993, when I was introduced to him as Kevin Powell from *The Real World,* he greeted me with: "Whassup dogg! I had your back on that show, man!" There I was a fan of his, and he was a fan of mine, too. On some level we resonated with each other across our different struggles, and the activist in me was drawn to his story. He had pure talent and genius as an artist, and his mother, Afeni Shakur, had been a member of the Black Panther Party in the 1960s and early 1970s. She was imprisoned during part of her pregnancy with Tupac. Given his revolutionary roots, it's not surprising that he became a dynamic spokesperson for the hip-hop nation, for young Black males, and for young America. He was well versed in issues of the day, and he gave back to the community tirelessly. When the youth vote became a hot topic during the 1990s, Tupac proposed that if the almost ten million young people in his and Snoop Dogg's fan base combined and actually voted, young America could change the world. Yet, the ironic tragedies of his life—the disturbing criminal charges leveled against him and his nearly year-long imprisonment for sexual assault—were problematic on many levels. Witnessing Tupac's experiences motivated me to begin rethinking American manhood away from patriarchy, sexism, and violence. He remains the most fascinating interview subject of my career.

When confronted with the challenges and battles of our generation like those that Tupac faced, I sometimes felt extremely guilty for not being a full-time activist and organizer. I wrestled with the idea that I had given my life over to pop culture, but in retrospect, this period was extremely important in shaping my subsequent work. I was learning new ways to reach people, particularly young Americans, around social issues. For example, it was widely believed that General Colin Powell could become America's first Black president if he mounted a campaign. So, when the 1996 presidential election arrived, I encouraged *Vibe* to start a new political section entitled "Get Up on It," and I interviewed the former chairman of the Joint Chiefs of Staff (Powell's position at the time).

In my work at *Vibe* and my role on *The Real World* I saw how pop culture was changing politics and activism in our nation. Gone were the days of mainly relying on grassroots efforts as an organizing tool. Mobilizing young people also required a working knowledge of contemporary music, media, magazines, and social networks. We saw a glimpse of this during Bill Clinton's 1992 campaign when he played the saxophone on *The Arsenio Hall Show* and spoke with young voters at a televised MTV townhall meeting. What we were creating in the 1990s, without realizing its significance, was the framework for twenty-first-century activism and volunteerism: a merging of politics and pop culture combined with a savvy use of new technologies.

Diverse groups of young people came together as never before in this developing era of activism. As evidenced by the eclectic gathering of personalities on that first season of *The Real World*, the "MTV generation" was more diverse than any before it. The pages of *Vibe* magazine illustrated it perfectly: Hip-hop was uniting youth from every walk of life. With a shared cultural aesthetic, we of different social, ethnic, and economic backgrounds sampled the earlier movements for political empowerment and launched our own. In many ways, the Obama campaign represents the fulfillment of this transformation. The iconic campaign image of Barack Obama by graffiti artist Shepard Fairey is just one example of how youth culture, innovative new media, and online social networks spurred young people to action across this nation. The massive waves that responded showed the potential of a truly multicultural movement in America: crowds of Obama supporters—White, Black, Latino, Asian, Native American, female, male, straight, gay, all classes, all faiths—the hip hop generation, bolstered by those who came behind us, rallied with those who came before us. Mashed together, chanting in unison "Yes, we can" or "Si, se puede," the crowds we saw at President Obama's inauguration and throughout the 2008 campaign revealed the undeniable truth I came to believe in the 1990s: We can create multicultural coalitions to achieve justice and full equality in our nation. The possibilities of who we are and what we can be have been there all along. Just a simple spark was needed to ignite the revolution within.

But the challenge for you, young America, now that Barack Obama is the president, is to not allow this spark, this newfound activism, to go the way of an outdated social media tool or cell phone. We need to be clear that the Obama campaign was not the movement. To paraphrase the great actor and activist Danny Glover, the Obama phenomenon was a series of great moments and great events linked across America by raw emotion and a sense of purpose. The seed of a movement is what made his campaign possible and what continues in the aftermath of his victory. A movement by definition is the mass energy of people for one great social cause or another over the course of time. A movement is not about getting one person elected to office. It is about changing the lives of many people. Young America, I say these things to you because I have been struck by how many of us seem to believe that Barack Obama's presidency happened of its own accord, or that it will magically transform our country. It's as if people think his story only belongs to these times. If that were the case, then why were so many elder Americans of all races weeping tears of joy on election night? It is because regardless of our collective achievement on Tuesday, November 4, 2008, like me, they never thought they'd live to see something like this. They believed it fundamentally impossible that a Black person, a biracial person, a person with America's grand tradition of diversity and multiculturalism embedded in the marrow of his bones, would actually one day ascend to the highest office in the land and, without question, on planet Earth.

Indeed, so many African Americans were hoping that Barack Obama would not win. Their heavy sighs and looks of profound concern would say, *Remember what happened to Black leaders like Medgar Evers, Malcolm X, and Dr. King.* That fear is still there now, because despite their best efforts, our parents and our grandparents cannot forget the long saga we call American history. I agree with you wholeheartedly, young America, that fear, hatred, violence, poverty, and a contaminated environment are entirely unbecoming of the most powerful nation in the world. My own mother, when I asked her if she thought she'd experience a day like this, was mad blunt: "Maybe never" was her response. You must understand that my mother, conceived in a South Carolina shack in 1943, was bred into that dishonorable, fearful America where it was normal to see signs that read FOR COLOREDS ONLY and FOR WHITES ONLY. And it was not just the signs that were quite visible everywhere. It was the signs in people's minds that ultimately blocked her from obtaining anything better than a grade-school education. She was forced to begin working at age eight, picking cotton for the wealthy White folks in her dusty little South Carolina town. Those signs in people's minds ultimately led her, and two of her siblings, to flee the South. Challenging that version of America, they packed up for Jersey City, where I was born and raised.

So we need to be clear that Americans like my mother represent an era, a generation in which the very thought of a Barack Obama becoming president was beyond the realm of sanity. The insanity that is American racism made the average quest for a better life a sheer impossibility. I wonder, matter-of-factly, what my mother aspired to be when she was a little girl, if she had any hope of a better life, of doing great and historic things herself, if she believed she could transcend the racism, yes, but also the sexism and the classism that engulfed her from birth. This ordinary American, my mother, has, in her lifetime, been called "nigga," "coon," "jigaboo," "lazy," "shiftless," and "welfare queen," and these are some of the kinder words. Americans like my mother know this country better than any of us ever will. She knows what is on the flesh, and she knows what is beneath the surface, in the underbelly of our journey together. Nothing in her life, nothing in her worldview, could have predicted the election of Barack Obama. Nothing.

But ordinary people, throughout history, have always achieved extraordinary goals, so it needs to be stated and restated until it lodges into our hearts and minds: Had it not been for all the ordinary people like my mother, Mr. Obama would not be president, and this most powerful nation on the planet would still be stuck in a pathetic state of arrested development, our "democracy" weakened by our inability to get past, well, the past. So we owe a great debt to those ordinary people, Black, White, Latino, Asian, Christian, Muslim, Jewish, all faiths who marched, sat in, rode buses, stood up to water hoses, guns, billy clubs, prison sentences, and the like so that we could be a better nation, under whichever God we choose to believe in. And President Obama's election is as much a culmination of their sacrifices as it is the hard-won victory of many whose names we do know: Fannie Lou Hamer, Ella Baker, Dr. King, Malcolm X, Rosa Parks, the Student Nonviolent

Coordinating Committee, the National Association for the Advancement of Colored People, the Southern Christian Leadership Conference, the National Urban League, the Congress of Racial Equality, the Black Panther Party, and the martyrs: those four little Black girls in a Birmingham, Alabama, church; two Jews and a Black man named Andrew Goodman, Michael Schwerner, and James Chaney; a White female civil rights volunteer named Viola Liuzzo; and all whose blood, sweat, and tears drove us closer to the freedom and equality we're still fighting for.

The struggle that brought us to this historical moment did not begin with the civil rights movement. For instance, this year marks the one-hundredth anniversary of the National Association for the Advancement of Colored People. We know the NAACP as an organization linked to the rights and progress of African Americans. What many of us do not know is that this organization had the same kind of multicultural coalition—Blacks and Whites coming together to form the group in February 1909—that propelled Barack Obama to the presidency. Whenever we have chosen to see our individual and collective humanity, we have inched forward this great democratic experiment in spite of America's racist history. So when we Generation Xers and Yers talk about the Obama age, we cannot afford to be arrogantly dismissive of that which made it possible. If there were no NAACP, there would have been none of the landmark Supreme Court victories, like *Brown v. the Board of Education of Topeka, Kansas,* nor all the smaller victories, in lower courts, long since forgotten. Had there been no civil rights movement, there would not have been the Civil Rights Act of 1964 nor the Voting Rights Act of 1965, major legislation that formed the foundation for the record voter turnouts in November of 2008.

President Obama's path was cleared not only by the civil rights movement and all the freedom-fighters who came before it, but also by post–civil rights era Americans, a majority of whom became much more comfortable with people of color in positions of leadership, authority, and influence. We owe this gradual and subtle change to a wave of images of Blacks in the mainstream including the brand of pop culture exemplified by *Vibe*, *The Real World*, and the hip-hop generation. Over the past two decades, *The Cosby Show*, Maya Angelou, Michael Jordan, Oprah Winfrey, Tiger Woods, Will Smith, Beyoncé, and, yes, all the iconic hip-hop figures like Tupac Shakur, P. Diddy, Jay-Z, Kanye West, and Lil Wayne have slowly but dramatically dismantled the COLOREDS ONLY, WHITES ONLY signs in our collective American psyche. And I must add that there is no question that Michael Jackson's *Thiller* — its record-shattering sales, its now classic and trailblazing videos —

not only made him the dominant music superstar on the planet, but also, arguably, laid the foundation for Barack Obama's global mass appeal. So we are now witnessing a generation that has been under the influence of mainstream Black role models for their entire lives come of age. The use of pop culture as a political force was a simple but radical approach. Little did we know how remarkable the change it achieved would be, especially given our very checkered and disturbing history around race.

Still, in early 2009, Eric Holder, President Obama's attorney general, suggested we are "a nation of cowards" for not having the courage to deal directly, once and for all, with our nation's legacy of racism. I happen to agree with Mr. Holder, and I don't

PRESIDENT OBAMA'S VICTORY WAS NOT THE GRAND FINALE OF DR. KING'S "DREAM," BUT IN ACTUALITY, AN ANNOUNCEMENT THAT THE REAL WORK HAS JUST BEGUN.

feel it contradicts my desire for a progressive, multicultural coalition in America. We need an emotionally honest and raw national dialogue about our past. We need people to work together for this—ordinary people, who have the guts to get past their own pains, traumas, and hurt feelings. And, by God, we need to love each other. In spite of Barack Obama's presidency, the business of ending American racism remains unfinished. If this were not the case, how do we explain an early twenty something Black male named Oscar Grant being shot in the back by a White police officer, at point-blank range, while on the ground at a Bay Area train station? He had no weapon nor was he resisting arrest. In fact he was pleading for mercy, referencing his little daughter. Mr. Grant was shot and killed just three weeks before Barack Obama's historic inauguration, and the outcry was so heavy in Oakland that young people took to the streets smashing windows and flipping parked cars. I do not condone the reactive violence, but I understand it. The violence was those young people's way of saying, yes, Mr. Obama is in the White House, but that does not mean we are in a post racial America. Post racial should mean, among other things, that no people should ever feel that they can lose their life anytime they cross paths with a police officer because that police officer, regardless of race or creed, views them as a menace to society, as animalistic, as not worthy of basic human love and respect.

And to this now centuries-old struggle of race and racism in America, we must add some observations about the current state of affairs President Obama has inherited. There are the endless and unimaginably costly wars in Iraq and Afghanistan. There is the everywhere and nowhere war on terrorism. At home we have one of the worst financial crises in our nation's history. I have never heard of so many searching for jobs or losing their businesses and homes. They are utterly terrified that it may be their turn to fall through the trapdoor formerly known as the American dream. Indeed, if getting an education is the American dream, then what does it mean that the twenty-first-century-education means years of debt and the inability to find work comparable to one's schooling? When property ownership feels more like a prison sentence than real freedom and empowerment, the dream has become a nightmare. The immeasurable depth of these challenges proves that President Obama's victory was not the grand finale of Dr. King's "dream" but in actuality an announcement that the real work has just begun.

The real work starts with the understanding that America is not the country it once was, but neither are we the country we can be. We need to ask ourselves this question: What would

America look like today if there had not been any effort to create inclusive definitions of freedom and democracy? We deceive ourselves mightily if we believe, in our naiveté, that Obama's presidency has miraculously ended our many problems and our many forms of discrimination, and political, economic, and gender oppression. A great symbolic victory, yes, but when it comes to America's social relations and the many crises confronting our nation, one man's victory does not change an entire political history or a sobering present reality. The real work is for you and I to do, young America. We must take up the causes of transforming our educational system; cleaning up our environment; closing the massive gap between the super wealthy and the super poor; ridding our society of all manner of violence; ensuring access to health care for all; seeing all Americans as our sisters, brothers, and members of the human family, regardless of color, hair texture, speech patterns, faith, gender, sexual orientation, or political ideology. In short, the real work must be about the forward march of time and the forward march of our souls.

That march once was accompanied by a civil rights–era song that proclaimed "ain't gonna let nobody turn me around." As I watched young America become enthralled by Barack Obama's campaign, I felt that, having captured the spirit of that song, we might just be ready and able to move into the next era and do the real work. The magic of this historical victory is that a determined, diverse army of us made it happen. We proved that the civil rights movement, the difficult and very slow integration of American schools and neighborhoods, and the pop-culture phenomena that followed did something to our very American psyches. In spite of ourselves, in spite of our history, in spite of our daily stumbles, we did not turn back. Instead, we became far more human than we could ever have believed possible. We grew morally averse to the ugly, visceral, in-your-face hatred that my mother's generation recalls as easily as their own first and last names. We finally learned the lesson that I missed as a young activist: Substantive progress is not possible without building bridges across multiracial and multicultural groups. Whether we are African Americans from the Old South, West Indians from the Caribbean, the First Nations who originally populated this land, Mexicans returning across American borders to ancestral homelands, or the scores of Europeans, Asians, and Africans who've come here voluntarily, as that civil rights song says, we cannot turn back to our divisive past. Young America, our resolve is strong, and if new victories are to be won, as we say in hip-hop, we must keep it moving. Forward. Our eyes firmly on that prize we've all been dreaming of.

We must realize that "We are the ones we have been waiting for." Barack Obama's successful presidential campaign reminded us of these now immortal words from the late poet June Jordan. Her message liberated us at a moment when we had become conditioned to believe that we were powerless. Over the past two decades we have been anaesthetized by a huge dose of leadership that was not really leadership at all: politicians, ministers, talk show pundits, and the like who were handpicked, ordained, elected, or appointed. Dr. King once warned us of such manufactured leadership, but still we allowed it to entrap us. Not only can we now affirm that these people are not leaders, we have also been inspired by President Obama's victory to know the truth: The power to lead is in our own hands both individually and collectively. Lead, as in changing the direction of the conversation or creating a new dialogue entirely. For Obama that meant refreshing our American memory with words like "hope" and "change" for a people whose lonely eyes have been resting on fear and despair for so long. Lead, as in creating or building a program, an organization, an institution, that services the people, any people. It does not take a rocket scientist to figure out what any given community needs to survive and, more importantly to win. You simply have to ask the people, and they will tell you. Lead, as in being accessible and available to the people, the community, the humans you claim to serve or want to help. This means you know the ways and culture of the community you serve; you know their language, their food, their customs, their hopes, and their fears; and you love them without any pre-conditions. This means you earn their love and their respect because you serve them, not the other way around.

It is this spirit of leadership that speaks to the best of who we are as Americans, a truly global people. We know, collectively, that we are so much more than racists, sexists, classists, homophobes, religious bigots, religious zealots, raging provocateurs, or perpetrators of violence. There is goodness in us all, if we are willing to sow, nurture, and grow that goodness. I honestly believe this, in spite of history's promise that moments like this one won't last very long. Movements and moments in history may come and go, but if we, the leaders of this era, can make helping our fellow human being as critical to our lives as whatever God, higher power(s), or values we say we believe in, then what we experienced in 2008 will become something we can sustain for the remainder of our natural lives. My challenge to you, young America, is that you accept this mantle of leadership, that you make of it what you will, even if you sometimes travel the road alone. Find in your heart and soul something you love, something you are passionate about, something you are willing to use your voice for, and change it for the better. Engage your life fully, be courageous enough to fall down and get back up. Be so idealistic as to believe that, yes, you can save this world of ours from itself. But don't forget to save yourself. Take care of yourself holistically, as you work to take care of and help others.

Do not do what I was guilty of in my youth and run away from what you feel now; do not fear it, avoid it, or pass it off to someone else as I did. Those are the great regrets of my younger years. I wrestled so much with my own self-esteem, yes, with loving myself and others, that I missed many opportunities to be an agent for change. I did not fully grasp the love and the power I had in my hands. Love in the very basic and tender sense that it takes an enormous emotional capacity to actually want to do public service, to help others to be free and empowered, to give back. Just the thought of it is love manifested. Be courageous enough to love those who make you comfortable and even those who make you uncomfortable. And, without a doubt, love those you may not like, or who you know do not like you. If the world is to change, one human at a time, we must practice what Dr. King called a dangerous kind of selflessness. We must love ourselves and each other as though the universe's very existence depends upon it.

You live in a world that I could not have imagined when I was a twenty something just two decades ago. I never actually expected Jesse Jackson to become president, even in 1988 when he amassed millions of votes and for one brief moment actually was ahead for the Democratic nomination. With Barack Obama's victory you accomplished something in your youth that none of us thought possible: An underdog, outsider candidate would become president of our country. You did it and we did it. You did it, we did it, by believing in something even when older Americans were walking the safe route. You did it, we did it, because we were bold enough to lead our elders, our parents; bold enough to be the leaders we've been ordained to be. You did it, we did it, by believing in the strength of our diversity. You did it, we did it, by going door to door, the old-school way. You did it, we did it, by volunteering our time to register people to vote, in the spirit of all those young Americans who registered people to vote during the civil rights era. You did it, we did it, by using the social networks, e-blasts, text messaging, and by responding en masse to MoveOn.org's, GenerationEngage's, and ColorOfChange.org's mobilization strategies to rally Americans, especially young Americans, from Brooklyn to Berkeley, from Harlem to Hawaii.

Those facts give me hope. With more young Americans voting in last year's presidential election than in any other time in history, I now have hope that our nation can go forward when the mass energy of the people is brought to bear on current affairs. But I ask, with all love and respect for you, that you do not become disillusioned like some in my generation, now in our thirties and forties. Voting on Tuesday, November 4, 2008, is simply not enough. Once more, we cannot entertain the illusion that Barack Obama's election means we have finally arrived at Dr. King's promised land. Obama is neither a savior nor the savior. In fact, it is very rare that a politician has created dramatic changes in American history, save Lincoln's Emancipation Proclamation, Roosevelt's New Deal, and Johnson's Great Society. More often than not, change comes from the people and infiltrates the corridors of power, not the other way around. Lincoln's words would not have occurred were it not for the abolitionists. Roosevelt's vision would not have become clear were it not for the workers, the artists, and the activists. Johnson's Civil Rights Act of 1964, Voting Rights Act of 1965, and War on Poverty would not have been made possible without Dr. King's moral authority, Ella Baker's organizing, Fannie Lou Hamer's priceless courage, and Malcolm X's bravado. And Obama's change will not be possible without your making volunteerism, organizing, and political and social awareness as natural to your being as breathing. The worst possible thing any of us could do is become complacent and, victory now won, not vote on a consistent basis—from school board elections to presidential elections—for the remainder of our natural lives. The worst possible thing any of us could do is believe that change is now in the hands of our leaders, expecting them to be the change agents we want to see here, everywhere, now.

And so it is for you, young America, to cease to quote historical figures and to start to make your own history in these times. There are two types of people on the planet: those who make things happen, and those who wait for things to happen. I am especially talking to those of you who are teenagers and twenty somethings. Some amongst my generation think we are wiser because of years. I respectfully disagree. There may be wisdom in some quarters, but you possess something that is immeasurable: You have the daring to believe in freedom because you have not yet been corrupted by politics, by people who lack morality and spirituality, yet pretend to be leaders—like the assemblyman from my Brooklyn community who told me publicly that I did not understand "the pathways to leadership." Do not let anyone tell you that there is only one pathway to become a leader, to be an agent for change. Barack Obama would have never defeated Hillary Clinton in the Democratic primaries had he followed some pathway to leadership. He invoked the vision and courage to throw out the rules and buck the system. Obama is not the exception to the rule. His achievements are not beyond the possibilities for you. Young America, we the people of this nation, and this world need you all to be the leadership we are waiting for. Find your passion, find your cause, locally and nationally, and keep it moving; don't turn back. If not you, then who, and if not now, then when?

Yours truly,

Kevin

OPEN LETTER TO
Congressman Ed Towns

Friday, July 4, 2008

Dear Congressman Towns:

I hope you and your family are well.

I am forced to write this open letter because you have failed to stand up and be counted during this election. After a quarter century you have also not delivered for the people in your district. I am disappointed because I had thought that a senior politician such as yourself, a twenty-five-year-veteran of Congress, would be more than happy to participate in our nation's democratic process and agree to a debate in the venue of your choice. The condition of the district and your track record may have motivated you to stay away from the spotlight with the hope that you could just manage to squeak by and get back into office for yet another term.

But rather than meet me face-to-face to discuss the issues and challenges we have as a nation, you have chosen the low road. Please allow me to remind you that this path is wide and has led many of our politicians to perdition. Your attempts to discredit my campaign for Congress by personal attacks and character assassination will not work. The people of Brooklyn are tired of the same old political tricks. They demand a change. Instead of recognizing the needs of the people you are supposed to represent, you have chosen to tell lies about me and to distort my life to make me seem like some sort of criminal.

These underhanded tactics are disturbing to me on so many levels. I really didn't expect this from you. I thought that you, someone born in North Carolina in the early 1930s, during the era of legal segregation, would know better than most how it feels to be treated in such a rude and disrespectful manner. And as someone who participated in our civil rights movement, I thought you would remember that the whole point of that struggle was to create a level playing field so that future generations of African Americans would be able to pursue their lives and their dreams in liberty and happiness.

I challenge you, Congressman Towns, to five public debates, any time and any place, to talk about the real issues facing the people of Brooklyn:

The War in Iraq
Education
Health Care
Violence in the Community
The Environment
Jobs and the Economy
Gender Equality
Immigration

YOU NEED TO COME TO THE COMMUNITY, WITH SOME IDEAS, PROGRAMS, OR BILLS TO SERIOUSLY ADDRESS THE PROBLEMS IN BROOKLYN This campaign has given me the opportunity to share my vision for the future of Brooklyn and America. I have done my best, with my staff, to put together wide-ranging information, legislation, and new proposals on many areas of concern to our district and nation. In fact, we are calling our action agenda The Plan: A New Way for the Twenty-First Century. I am not naïve enough to believe that I will get to Washington and single-handedly swing the legislature. But by doing the work and with the right information, I will be able to vote knowledgeably on the bills before me while always remembering that every vote is for the people of Brooklyn, not for my political and financial carriers.

I plan to use my office and the resources it provides to bring help to the district. And I plan to help educate my congressional peers and other leaders about some new and innovative ways to approach our problems and what I have learned from the many people I have worked with over the years. I will also make use of my skills developed as a community organizer for more than twenty years since I was a teenage activist. I have a great ability to bring people and groups together who can work to solve cooperatively some of the problems we face. The formal congressional committee structures are not the only way work gets done in government. I am committed to on-the-ground action in my community and not simply legislating from Washington. As a progressive public servant, I have no other choice but to think and act outside the box, always, to be the kind of leader who will do whatever it takes to empower people so that they can empower themselves.

I challenge you to come up with something more than tired phrases; you need to come to the community, with some ideas, programs, or bills to seriously address the problems in Brooklyn. Moreover, I ask you and your staff and your family members and circle of associates to deal in facts, to tell the truth when describing me, your opponent—and to refrain from the kind of personal attacks and distortions that people are no longer willing to tolerate.

It has come to my campaign's attention that you, your staff, your family members and associates have been referring to me as a "woman beater" and suggesting that I have spent time in jail.

Once and for all, I am going to set the record straight, for your own information—since you like to tell the media that you do not know me—and for the information of the good people of Brooklyn, and of America. Ironically, it is members of the media who have tipped me off, time and again, to your efforts to demonize me in hopes of winning yet another reelection.

I find it fascinating that you say, again and again, that you do not know me. For most of the nearly twenty years I have lived in New York, I have lived here in Brooklyn's Tenth Congressional District—your district. I have been an active member in this community, running forums, town-hall meetings, anti violence and mentorship programs. I frequently speak and conduct workshops in our community's schools, churches, and foster care programs, from Fort Greene to East New York and points in between. I belong to the Fort Greene Association, I attend Emmanuel Baptist Church, and I routinely support businesses in our community, like the Five Spot, like Karen's Body Beautiful, like Night of the Cookers. For several years now I have been working hard to improve the lives of the people in our district, and yet our paths have never crossed. In my travels around the district, I have learned that I am not the only one you don't know. Many of your constituents have noticed that you are not present in their lives in any meaningful way.

Even as I keep reaching out to members of the community and learning better who they are and what they need, you have closed two of your offices—during this campaign cycle—leaving many residents scratching their heads. After twenty-five years, the sad reality is that much of the district does not know who you are. You have failed to reach out to them; you have not effectively brought help and change to the lives of the people in the Tenth Congressional District. In short, you are out of touch.

So for your information, here are the facts:

First off, I have never spent a night in jail in my life.

Now let's address the second charge. You have called me a "woman beater." Violence was me, Mr. Towns. But let's not get stuck in the past, and let us never ignore the full story and context of any person's life. That is how we dehumanize each other, and as a man of God and someone keenly familiar with the Bible, I am sure you know better than that, and I am sure you know about personal redemption.

I was born and raised in Jersey City, New Jersey, to a young single Black mother, who was never married to my father. Indeed, my father so emotionally devastated my mother by his irresponsibility, absence, and neglect, that my mother turned that hurt on me, her only child. Yes, like many young people in your district, Mr. Towns, I was a victim of all manner of violence as a child, including physical and mental abuse. I strongly recommend that you Google my poem "Son2Mother" to get the full picture of what an inner-city child like me, born on the heels of the civil rights movement, had to live through in terms of violence and low self-esteem and feelings of worthlessness.

In spite of all the above, I was able to get a decent public school education, enough for me to see some glimmer of hope out of the poverty and misery of my youth. That is why public school education matters so much to me today.

But I am also very clear, today, that if you teach a child that violence is the only solution for conflict, then that child will become violent as an adult. We see that every single day here in Brooklyn. I see and hear the stories as I walk the streets of our community, listen to the children, the teens, the parents, the teachers. Violence, to paraphrase Dr. King, is the language of the unheard, the cry of the powerless. As an adult, in spite of my college education, in spite of moving to New York City and becoming a relatively successful writer, I became someone who had to battle my own feelings of powerlessness through a bad temper and violent outbursts against both men and women.

As I have done in my speeches all across America, in several of my eight books, in essays in *Essence* magazine in 1992 and in *Ms.* magazine in 2001, on the website huffingtonpost.com in 2008 (see my essay "Ending Violence against Women and Girls"), I have always spoken publicly, locally, nationally, in all forms of media, about my life's journey and my personal challenges. I have nothing to hide. Nothing. My life is an open book, a testimony of the possibilities of personal growth and redemption and change if one is willing to do the hard work.

So once again, for the record—yes, between the years of 1987 and 1991, I did have a pattern of violence against women. And, it took me even longer to control my temper and aggression toward other men. But thanks to years of therapy, spiritual development, and personal evolution and the support and encouragement of women like bell hooks, Susan Taylor, Pearl Cleage, Dr. Johnnetta Cole, and Gloria

Steinem, I have moved beyond that destructive behavior to become a profeminist, antisexist man committed to gender equality and nonviolent conflict resolution. I have worked alongside males like Michael Kimmel, Byron Hurt, Jelani Cobb, and Charles Knight in trying to craft new ideas of American manhood not rooted in domination, violence, homophobia, fear, and confusion.

GIVE PEOPLE THE OPPORTUNITY TO IMAGINE THE UNIMAGINABLE. American males have been taught some dangerous lessons over the generations. We have been taught to hide and suppress our emotional responses to personal troubles. This emotional pressure is often released in violent and self-destructive behavior. Coming to grips with the realities of victimization has been the greatest challenge of my life. Looking for one's own flaws is never easy and it hurts even more when you find them. I cannot even begin to count, Mr. Towns, how many people in Brooklyn as well as other parts of New York City—indeed, all across America—have said that my testimony gives them hope for all the poor, disenfranchised men and boys out there. But only if we are willing to be honest and accountable for all our actions. That is what a leader, a public servant, is supposed to do: Give people the opportunity to imagine the unimaginable. The realization that I could change and redeem my own life and those of the people around me has led me to community organizing full time, to being a public servant for the remainder of my life. I could not think of anything that brings me greater joy and fulfillment than helping people, all people. My most recent work includes the following:

I organized approximately seven hundred college students into something called Katrina on the Ground, which did relief work in the Gulf Coast after the devastating storm.

I routinely participate in organizing efforts around affordable housing, around the subprime mortgage crisis, around quality educational options for our youth, and many other quality-of-life issues for our communities, like health care, a cleaner environment, and more resources for social programs instead of the war in Iraq.

Just this past spring, I was honored to participate in the United Nations global campaign to end violence against women and girls, and I have also worked with Amnesty International on this issue. If the United Nations and Amnesty International know that I am no "woman beater," and have brought me in as a spokesperson to reach males and females in the global community, then why can't you and your circle of supporters see that, sir?

Here in Brooklyn, I have been a part of private sessions with gang members, many of whom live right in the Tenth

Congressional District, helping to educate them about the destructiveness of violent behavior against each other and against women and girls.

We held a national conference on Black males, right here in Brooklyn in your district in June 2007, with three thousand attendees. That gathering turned into a monthly Black male empowerment workshop, which attracts older and younger Black men from New York, New Jersey, and other parts of the metro area.

All of this work around Black male development will culminate with a practical self-help book, entitled *The Black Male Handbook: A Blueprint for Life.* I encourage you to pick up a copy. I am the editor of this book, sir, and it offers practical ways that

I AM SO DETERMINED TO MAKE SURE THAT AMERICAN MALES, BLACK AMERICAN MALES, DO NOT MAKE THE MISTAKES I MADE IN MY PAST LIVES.

Black males of all ages can develop spiritual foundations, become politically involved, learn about our great cultural traditions, become healthier physically and mentally, and rid ourselves of violent tendencies, against other males, against females. Nothing like this book currently exists, and I was only able to create *The Black Male Handbook* with the help of contributors like the actor Hill Harper, BET's Jeff Johnson, and the brilliant young financial wiz Ryan Mack, because of all that I have overcome in my own life. I am so determined to make sure that American males, Black American males, do not make the mistakes I made in my past lives. There is no way to do that without being the kind of leader who is an open book, entirely. And there is no way to do that without being a mentor, a guide, in some form or fashion. If one is placed in a leadership position, then one must lead. There are no excuses, no easy paths to leadership. It is a calling, as we say in the church.

Moreover, my point is that we have to do more than just talk about the issues and challenges facing our communities. We must do something to bring about change. That is what I have always worked for: action and solutions. Anything less would mean that we are simply stagnating and wasting our time on Earth.

Unfortunately you have chosen not to see any of this work, Mr. Towns, even though I once had a meeting with your daughter, Deirdre, to talk about her help with my annual holiday party and clothing drive to benefit homeless young people. Your own daughter, sir, knew who I was, knew my work as a community organizer, knew that I was a founding staff member at *Vibe*, that I appeared on the very first season of MTV's *The Real World*; and your daughter knew that I had a voice that people respect and listen to, because I had earned that respect. But do you even talk with your own children about the leaders of their generation? You can always ask them what is happening now, on the streets of the community you claim to represent.

But, alas, it appears that you do not, and perhaps that is why the Tenth Congressional District has been stuck in a state of arrested development for so long. We can no longer afford to wait for things to happen. We must take bold action and put in the hard work that is required to change the current situation.

So, again, Mr. Towns, you say that you do not know me. You have failed to see my work and the work of others going on right under your nose. How many other community organizations and community leaders struggling for that little bit of assistance they so justly deserve are simply not in your field of vision?

But I can see you, and so can the good people of Brooklyn.

We see that you are mostly interested in keeping your comfortable congressional seat. We see that you have raised more than 60 percent of your campaign funds from PACs and lobbyists. We see that you invited Congressman JC Watts—a Republican aligned with President George W. Bush and his neoconservative agenda—to raise money for your campaign against me.

It seems that you are willing to win even at the price of destroying the reputation of another man, a Black man young enough to be your own son. In fact, I am your son, as are all the Black males of the Tenth Congressional District. Some of us stand on street corners every single day, wondering

DO YOU EVER SPEAK TO THESE YOUNG BLACK MALES IN YOUR DISTRICT? DO YOU KNOW THEIR NAMES? DO YOU EVEN CARE ABOUT THEIR LIVES, SIR?

where our lives are going—other than prison or an early death. We are all the Black males who seek employment and education, only to be let down by failed public schools and a lack of basic life and job skills. Do you ever speak to these young Black males in your district? Do you know their names? Do you even care about their lives, sir?

One of your former staffers recently told me that you long since stopped caring. He said that in the 1960s and 1970s, you cared, but that over time you drifted away from the mission of the civil rights movement. He said that you cared less about the people, and more about making sure that your family and your circle of friends were taken care of. He said that you have become a caricature of a Black leader, that you now see your congressional seat as a family business, to be passed on to your son or daughter-in-law, with no regard for democracy or the public good. His words saddened me deeply.

Are these words true? If so, then your so-called leadership is a slap in the face of all the women and men, all the girls and boys, who marched and died during the civil rights era so that you could have your congressional seat in the first place. Is that what you want your legacy to be? That few of your constituents knew your name or your face? That even fewer know of anything you've done to empower the people, to transform lives here in Brooklyn?

Mr. Towns, you have been in office for twenty-five years, with a paid staff of at least twenty people in New York City and Washington. But what do you, and more importantly the people of your district, have to show for it? You have had as many as four offices, so the residents of Brooklyn's Tenthth Congressional District find it unacceptable how little you've brought back to Brooklyn, how little you've done for our communities. Indeed, when out campaigning, most people we ask cannot name three, two, or even one significant thing that you have accomplished in your twenty-five years in office. Your seniority means very little given that, outside of Congressman Charles Rangel, you have the second-longest tenure of the New York City delegation, yet you do not chair a single House committee.

All of these are the reasons why I am challenging you, Congressman Towns, for your seat. In a democracy, no public servant, no elected official, no party leader, should be above being questioned, above being held accountable, or above being called to public debate on the issues of the day.

This is why individuals as different as George Soros; Chris Rock; his wife, Malaak Compton-Rock; and Gloria Steinem support my campaign. This is why we have a committee called Women for Kevin Powell, which includes more than one hundred diverse and influential women from Brooklyn, New York City, and across America. You can view the Women for Kevin Powell committee and their statement of support right at my campaign website. This is why, in fact, much of the leadership of my campaign is women. Feminist, progressive, no-nonsense women. Apparently they do not consider me a "woman beater." And, moreover, I apologized to those few women I violated nearly twenty years ago, and they have accepted my apology and forgiven me, as have all the males I have ever had conflict with, for the record. Human beings appreciate honesty, and they appreciate accountability. If a Malcolm X or a Bobby Kennedy, two of my heroes, could change, could grow, could learn to be fully human, self-critical, and accountable in their very short lives, why can't I? If they both could grow into world-class humanitarians, why can't I? Your attacking a younger male like me, with my background, says that you do not believe in any of us in Brooklyn, that you have no hope for any of us, that you see no possibilities for any of us, that we are all just annoyances to be attacked and discarded. Is that how you really feel about the men and boys who could easily be your sons and grandsons?

But there are those who do see me for who I am today, who do see me as a whole human being. This is why we have growing support within the netroots community, a growing group of activists who use the Internet—blogs, online media, and social networks—to stay connected. This is why as we walk the streets of Brooklyn, younger people and older people of all different backgrounds tell us it is time for honest leadership. This is why people tell me everyday they respect me, because I am real, I am accessible, and I am not above the people in any way. Their lives are my many lives. Their triumphs and tragedies are my many triumphs and tragedies.

Without question, the American people, here in New York and elsewhere, want leadership that is visionary, leadership that they can relate to, leadership that builds bridges, that gives people a chance at life, at the American dream. For sure, a leader should be doing one of three things, if not all three, on a consistent basis: changing the direction of tired conversations, or creating new ideas, new conversations; building institutions, organizations, or businesses that support and benefit a community; or working on the frontlines, there with the people, as often as possible. If someone in a leadership position does not do any of those things, then he or she is not a leader. He or she is merely a spokesperson, or a figurehead, or worse, a puppet for the interests of others outside the community.

Congressman Towns, my team and I will continue to run a clean and honest campaign. Your character

YES, THAT NEW WAY MEANS WE WANT REAL DEMOCRACY, AND WE WANT IT NOW attacks and dirty ploys are the politics of yesterday, of the age of political machines and backroom deals, of politicians who think it is their birthright to hold office either until they die or until it is time to pass the seat on to a family member. It is time for a new leadership in America, this much is clear. Generations X and Y, or the hip-hop generations, or whatever pundits like to call us, have awakened, and we finally realize how much power and clout we have. And we are going to use that power and clout to create the world we want to see. Tomorrow is today for us, and we are very clear it is our turn to lead.

I remember when I interviewed Tupac Shakur for *Vibe* back in the 1990s, he talked about the power he had just by virtue of all the millions of fans who bought his CDs. Well guess what, Mr. Towns? All of us who grew up on MTV and BET, all of us who vote on *American Idol,* all of us who download music from iTunes, all of us with handheld devices and MySpace and Facebook pages have networks that communicate in ways that were unimaginable when Tupac was alive. And we are using them to rally people around the terrible Sean Bell verdict, to rally people to vote and volunteer on campaigns, to speak out on the issues of our times. We respect and admire those who've come before us, but we want to lead in a new way. That new way will include street teams and netroots organizing. That new way will include remixing politics with marketing savvy and marching and protesting when necessary. That new way will include music and poetry and using our cell phones for political mobilization. And that new way will include creating an entire nation of small donors so that progressive candidates don't ever have to sell their souls just to be in politics. Yes, that new way means we want real democracy, and we want it now.

OPEN LETTER TO **Congressman Ed Towns**

Lastly, many of your former staffers and interns, in Brooklyn, and in Washington, D.C. have confirmed a common assumption about the workings of your office, your lack of vision, and your remarkably lax attitude about the challenges confronting Brooklyn. They have noted your preference for your homes in Washington or in Florida rather than your house on a hill here in Brooklyn.

Congressman Towns, you are a Christian, as I am, and you are an ordained minister. I can only assume that this means, somewhere in your soul, you can see what your community really looks like. But still I marvel at the staggering amount of inaction on your part. We stand today at a critical juncture in the journey of urban America. Your pleas for Barack Obama's endorsement will not get you the support you need to win this race. Neither will the last-minute town hall meetings nor your efforts to grab some media attention even, embarrassingly, while posing with disgraced baseball player Roger Clemens.

Mr. Towns, let's bring our campaigns before the people and let them hear what we each have to say. Let us debate and show the good people of Brooklyn that our campaigns really believe in the democratic process. And on Election Day, we can let the people decide what kind of leadership and what kind of community they want.

Respectfully,

Kevin Powell

2008 Democratic Candidate for
the U.S. House of Representatives
Tenth Congressional District, Brooklyn, New York

OPEN LETTER TO
An American Woman

Monday, May 18, 2009

Hello Kevin Powell:

I read one of your articles in Ebony *magazine's May issue. It really hit close to home. On March 29, 2009, I lost my best friend to domestic violence. Her name was Kewaii Rogers-Buckner. She was only thirty-one years old. Kewaii was gunned down in her home by her husband in front of their three children, ages twelve, eleven, and nine. This tragic event has devastated all of her family, friends, loved ones, and our community. During our senior year in high school (1996), I slowly started to notice small changes in her personality and her need to be with this person every time she got the chance. Everything she talked about revolved around him. At first, he seemed to be an okay guy, but after we graduated he began to show his true colors. He tried to control everything about her— the way she wore her hair, the way that she dressed, and the people she talked to. And over time, he isolated her from her close friends (myself included) and most of her family. It was very hard to watch someone you've known almost your whole life and loved so dearly get caught up in such a painful situation. We all tried to get her to leave, but it was almost as if he had complete mind control over her. He would tell her that we were just jealous and didn't want to see her happy. In my heart, I knew I lost my friend a long time ago. He knew that I was the closest friend she had, and he made sure that he kept us apart. For many years I lived with the fear that he would hurt her, and, sadly, my worst fear came true. Just days before her murder she sought an order of protection from her husband, and in her statement she wrote that she feared for her life. She did make prior attempts to leave, but he threatened to harm her parents and even his own children. I know in my heart that she didn't want to live that way and she felt that she was protecting her family if she stayed. There are so many women that are in that exact situation and are going through the same thing, living in an abusive situation. My plea is for them to get out, and get out now, because it is not going to get better. It will only get worse. Please get out while they have a chance, because my friend didn't. I just wanted to share a portion of Kewaii's story with you because I don't want her death to be in vain, and if it can save just one life, I know it won't be. I am so grateful and thankful that you are willing to stand up for women and be the voice that a lot of them are afraid to use. There are so many people who just turn a blind eye to things like this. Thank you so much. Please keep our families in your prayers.*

Sincerely,

Shallon Patton

Tuesday, May 19, 2009

Dear Shallon Patton:

It devastates me to have heard stories like yours so many times these past several weeks since I appeared on *The Oprah Winfrey Show*, and since that *Ebony* magazine article, "Men Can Stop Domestic Violence," appeared. Let me say, first, my most heartfelt sympathies and condolences to Kewaii's family, to her children, to you and your family, and to your entire community there in Wilkes-Barre, Pennsylvania. I can only begin to imagine the intense hurt and pain you must feel, given this recent tragedy. And I am not quite sure what I can actually say to help, truthfully. Violence against women and girls, in our nation, and throughout every part of this world, is, without question, completely out of control.

TERMS LIKE "YES WE CAN" AND "CHANGE" AND "HOPE" WILL FOREVER BE EMPTY AND STALE SLOGANS IF THEY DON'T, TOO, APPLY TO HALF THE WORLD'S POPULATION— WOMEN AND GIRLS

Sadly, the cycle of emotional and physical abuse that Kewaii suffered for years is so typical, so predictable. Doubly sad that when she finally decided to get help herself—the key thing for any woman being battered—not even a "temporary protection from abuse order" could spare her life. I am not in the slightest trying to be funny here, but I cannot tell you how many women have said to me, throughout America, that a restraining order is utterly useless. One woman, a survivor of domestic abuse, said at a community forum, her mouth dripping with both cynicism and sarcasm born of years absorbing blows from her then husband, asked this very pointed question: "What are we women supposed to do with a restraining order? Wave it at the man in hopes that he will stop beating us and run away?"

From what you described in your note to me, and from what I gathered from one of your local newspapers, Kewaii never stood a chance, as her husband thoroughly isolated her for so long. These lines are especially jarring: "Mr. Buckner is very adamant about keeping me in Pennsylvania. He consistently tells me that he will hurt me if I leave him. He takes all the keys to the vehicles that are in my name so I can't get away. He stated if I leave him he will find me and if he doesn't find me, he'll kill my parents." And we now know, Shallon, that Mr. Buckner pushed Kewaii down a flight of stairs in June of 2008, that he pulled a gun on her last October, firing one bullet that pierced the living room couch and remained lodged in the floor long after that gun had been discharged. Ms. Kewaii Rogers-Buckner added in the petition "I am afraid to sleep at night because he is very unstable and I don't know what he will do." And we know, in hindsight, what he will do, Shallon, because he has done it, murdered Kewaii in cold blood in front of her children. What nightmares must they be having presently and will have for the rest of their lives? Their father, the man who helped to conceive them, executing their mother as if she were an enemy combatant on some foreign battlefield. But, no, she was no stranger to him, indeed she loved him, loved him more than she loved herself and her own life, and for that she is gone, forever. This is about Kewaii and domestic violence, yes, Shallon, it is. But it is also about love and hate, about emotional abuse and mental illness, and it is about how we males have been socialized to equate manhood with inhuman perceptions of power, control, ego, violence, and, yes, death and destruction. And it is about the powers and possibilities women have, and have always had, to fight back, to organize, and to resist sexism in their lives. Terms like "Yes we can" and "change" and "hope" will forever be empty and stale slogans if they don't, too, apply to half the world's population—women and girls—in every way that you can imagine.

In that vein, Shallon, I want to respectfully disagree with you that I am doing anything remarkable or special. Or that

I am a voice for women. I am neither special, nor a voice for anyone other than myself. And just like most men in America, I too was taught, in school, at home, on the streets and playgrounds, at the churches I attended as a youth, and via popular culture, that to be a man is to forever be in a position of power and advantage over women and girls. That flawed concept of maleness meant not only dominating women or girls, but also having little to no regard for their health and wellness, for their safety, for their bodies, and as was the case with Kewaii's husband, for their lives. Not every single male acts out in this way, of course, but in an environment of nonstop violence, which is the sort of environment that produced me, it is almost inevitable that a man-child will become violent toward other males and toward females, as I did in days gone by. But, thanks to the grace of God, years and years of counseling, a lot of reading and critical self-reflection, and individuals in my community who could recognize my wounds and sought to aid rather than discard me, I changed, and now I am here, not only to tell my story as I did in that *Ebony* piece, but to get other men to rethink our definitions of manhood. To do something, anything, to show that we can be allies to women and girls in the struggle to end gender violence once and for all. And to listen to the voices of women, to believe in and support their leadership, across the board. We really have no other choice at this point, Shallon. Nor do we have any choice other than to continue to speak out, even when there is mad disagreement. For example, immediately after my appearance on *The Oprah Winfrey Show*, which was the second of two shows concerning domestic violence in America in light of the Chris Brown–Rihanna saga, I duly noted that while many women generally applauded my remarks about the issue, a very small percentage of men had anything positive to say to me directly. Privilege for certain groups of people is very real on this planet, and we men undoubtedly benefit from women and girls being relegated to second-class citizenship. More unsettling still are the number of men of all races, of all educational and class backgrounds, from America and abroad, who email me regularly, seeking to portray themselves as victims, who without fail say that women beat up men, too. Let's deal with this one straight ahead. Yes, certainly, there are cases of females physically assaulting males. But, heck, to be mad blunt, why would a man or a woman want to stay in a toxic relationship in the first place, if there is constant yelling and screaming, constant pushing and shoving, constant throwing of this or that object at each other, or blows being constantly exchanged? And back to my point: The numbers are overwhelmingly slanted toward males assaulting females. In fact, given that statistical reality, any man who makes that argument is just being, well, a liar, and worse, a coward, for suggesting that violence levels are the one area in which the genders are equal. They are not. One such man, a Christian minister whose name I do not care to say, invited me on his nationally syndicated radio show under the guise of applauding my *Oprah* appearance. He then proceeded to say that I "sounded like a female," that my points on behalf of women were "dumb," and that "way more women are emotional batterers of men." He said that women abusing men is the major crisis we need to address in America—or something to that effect. I was flabbergasted because this man has a radio show with a sizable audience and because he is the pastor of a church. And you and I both know, Shallon, that women far outnumber men at most churches in our nation. So what is this man saying to these women, his followers, about domestic violence, about rape and incest, about sexism and misogyny, when they seek counsel from him? And what perverse pleasure, pray tell, was he getting out of dissing me on his program? I believe at the root of this male ignorance and defiance around discussing violence against women and girls lies a bottomless hatred, not just for women and girls, or for themselves, but for life itself. Who better represents life than one's mother, grandmother, aunt, sister, niece, daughter, wife, girlfriend, partner, lover? And even if a woman or girl happens to hit a man or boy, or happens to be so tormented herself that she has what one male, responding to my *Ebony* piece, called "verbal diarrhea," I submit there is something completely lacking in reason and logic with how we define manhood if we males believe that the only response to a woman who upsets or unnerves us in some way is violence. Such a response suggests that we are brutes, that we are beasts, that we have not combed the depths of our minds or souls to find solutions to conflicts that are rooted in peace and nonviolence, that we have not yet learned to use our wits instead of our fists.

So, Shallon, in this era of "change," this is what we have inherited: That when it comes to women and girls and how they are treated in their daily lives, there really has been no change at all. Not yet, with miles to go before we can sleep. What happened to Kewaii, and the too-many-to-count females like Kewaii whose stories are never told, thus never known, represents a virtual prison based on their gender. As you indicated in your letter to me, Kewaii had been mentally incarcerated for years, dating back to high school. The regular thread in my conversations with women who are domestic violence survivors is their low self-esteem, a feeling that this man, this male partner, somehow validates their lives, their beings, even as this partner seeks to control or end their lives. When we talk about "domestic violence" against women and girls, I would submit that it is more than the actual laying of hands. We've got to extend the conversation to the invisible "hits" they take every single day of their lives, especially if they are undereducated women, or poor women, or women of color. So many women have never heard of terms like "feminist" or "womanist," will never read the writings of bell hooks, Gloria Steinem, Eve

Ensler, or Alice Walker. Quite the contrary, most women do exactly what the women in my own family do: make it happen from day to day, month to month, year to year, by whatever means they can create for themselves. I say this because, Shallon, just as you are grieving the loss of Kewaii, I am grieving the loss of my dear Aunt Pearlie Mae Powell, my oldest auntie and my mother's oldest sister. She, like Kewaii, never had a chance to do, be, or experience real freedom, or real power over her own life. My aunt died on Monday, September 15, 2008, just thirty minutes after midnight, and less than a week after I lost my campaign for Congress here in Brooklyn, New York. I was already drained, mentally, physically, and spiritually, from that contest, and when I received the call from my mother, it just took me completely out of my head. "Pearlie Mae is dead," she said, with no emotion whatsoever, in that same tone used exactly twenty years before, in 1988, when her mother, my grandmother, died: "Lottie is dead." There was just a kind of matter-of-factness that a life was gone, and thus began the ritual, passed from generation to generation, of slowing the time and pausing our lives in that very moment, packing our suitcases, and returning to Southern soil for the "going home" ceremony. This ceremony would mark the passing of another woman for whom poverty or powerlessness or both had become a prison.

My aunt had been sick (or sickly, as my folks in South Carolina like to say) for years, but her body had been brutally attacked in the last year of her life by diabetes, leading to kidney failure and a full-time nursing home. Death is not something many of us ever want to think about, honestly, and I had pushed to the hidden vaults of my mind my mother telling me in December 2007 that my aunt's time might be near. I tried to shut out the awful reality of her impending death because when a loved one passes away, be it a horrific murder or the horrific toll a disease takes on the body, it forces us to examine our own life, our own mortality, the brief interval we each are given on this Earth. And when I think of my Aunt Pearlie Mae's life, which began November 25, 1939, in a two-room shack with her father and mother, I realize that she never really had a chance at an existence beyond poverty and the triple-pronged violence of racism, sexism, and classism.

It has been said that my aunt was born "afflicted," that she was "slow," and that in addition to her emotional abnormalities, she would never be able to have children of her own. Indeed, of my grandparents' five children, four girls and one boy, my Aunt Pearlie Mae was the only one who never left the nest and never delivered children. She lived with my grandparents until they were gone—my grandfather in the early 1970s, and my grandmother in the late 1980s. I cannot even imagine the traumas my aunt endured, on a May day in 1988 when my grandmother, still in the backwoods clapboard home they shared for years, succumbed to a massive heart attack and died. For my grandmother was my aunt's anchor, her source of strength, her connection to reality, her purpose for living, and then Grandma Lottie, as we called her, was dead. Aunt Pearlie Mae was nearly fifty and, abruptly, thrust into the world, alone. Yes, my Uncle Lloyd was there in the area, but he had his own demons to battle, and he would eventually wind up spending time in prison. My mother and her other two sisters were up North, their lives as Southerners long abandoned by a need to be, well, free, of the Old South and how it had held them captive. So Aunt Pearlie Mae moved to the only housing project in Ridgeland, South Carolina, and made a new life for herself. I do not know if she ever had a love or a lover in her life; if she had many friends; if she ever experienced prolonged periods of joy and happiness or, like many in my family tree, including me, if she suffered through bouts of depression and loneliness.

During my trips to South Carolina in her final years, I recall my aunt as forever childlike, but quick to anger, and paranoid about everything around her, perhaps because of those enduring emotional problems. Indeed, my Aunt Pearlie Mae collected some form of disability from the government her entire life, did not get much schooling, and spoke with the thick, molasses-like dialect of the Low Country Geechee folk from South Carolina. I always loved how she would say "umble" instead of "humble" when she spoke of individuals who had humility and respect for her. And I knew that Aunt Pearlie Mae took pride in her siblings' children. Perhaps she considered us nieces and nephews the children she never had.

It was at my aunt's wake, Shallon, at Sauls Funeral Home in Ridgeland, that fragments of my aunt's life drifted back to me. She loved to walk. She loved to laugh. She loved to call other women's babies ugly, in jest. Mostly family members were there at the wake until an elderly White woman, whose name I cannot recall, came up. She was older than my aunt, nearly eighty, but in good health. This woman was a volunteer at Aunt Pearlie Mae's last residence, the Ridgeland Nursing Center, I believe it is called. As she told her fond memories of my aunt, her eyes welled up and she called her "My little Pearlie Mae," because my aunt, a tiny woman, barely five feet tall, had grown frail in the last year of her life. She fought valiantly, held on a year longer than expected, then finally died of a heart attack in that nursing home bed while sleeping. And to learn that her life insurance policy was barely worth $5,000 was simply too much for me. It was a policy that had been sold to my grandparents and their children, at varying amounts

WE COMMUNITY ORGANIZERS FIND IT FAR EASIER TO HELP INDIVIDUALS REMOVED FROM THE CORE OF OUR LIVES BECAUSE WE CAN BE COMPASSIONATE WHILE KEEPING A PROFESSIONAL DISTANCE WHEN IT COMES TO OUR DEEPEST EMOTIONS between $5,000 and $10,000 because it was assumed, I suppose, that the lives of poor people from the rural South were not worth much more than this. We family members had to pool our money to cover the burial expenses and buy flowers. Anyone amongst us who says there is no poverty in this country, who says that I exaggerate the human suffering we have on these American shores should simply visit any small country town, or any big urban city, on any given day and witness for themselves how much it costs just to lay down and die. When I went with my uncle to my aunt's room at that nursing home, I was struck by the few remnants of her life stuffed into the drawers of a single dresser: photos of her sisters and brothers and nieces and nephews at various stages of our lives; a couple of jet-black wigs; cheap, dime-store jewelry; undergarments; her Sunday-best dresses for church; and a few legal documents confirming that she had actually, miraculously, existed for nearly seventy years.

It was agreed that I would deliver the family comments on Aunt Pearlie Mae at the funeral inside St. Matthew's Baptist Church. I did the best I could to summarize my aunt's life, to give her in death the praise and adulation I am sure she never received in her life. And I cried throughout the service because I was so extremely sad that there was nothing I could do, at this stage, to spare my aunt's life, to be able to see her one last time, alive. My God, the pangs of guilt foot-stomped inside my stomach. I sat in that church pew and listened to one mournful song after another, asking myself, how I could do this community development work for people, mostly strangers, wherever and whenever they needed assistance, but not call my aunt for more than a year, not make an attempt to see her, knowing the pain she was suffering through? Perhaps somewhere in our subconsciousness, we community organizers find it far easier to help individuals removed from the core of our lives because we can be compassionate while keeping a professional distance when it comes to our deepest emotions. We can erect a wall to shield ourselves from the daily slings and arrows associated with grassroots activism. At least that is what I have done, many times, through the years. But when it comes to our own family life, oh, how we avoid the unavoidable. Oh, how we ignore the fact that our families suffer through the very same social ills as others on this planet, because to confront our families means confronting ourselves. To confront our families is to confront our histories, the miracle of our lives, and in spite of all, it is to confront the solitary confinement of death. It is to confront our very imperfect selves, stark naked before our families, terrified that they will say something that will expose us for the actors we all are beyond the gated enclave of our family bonds. When it was time to shut and seal the casket on Aunt Pearlie Mae's body, I was confronted with the sad fact that all the work I do for my community, all the activism in the world, could not alleviate the pain and suffering of her life. My sadness and guilt climaxed as the small but enchanting choir, led by my cousin Renee on piano, launched into a song I had never heard before,

"I'm Free":

I'm free

Praise the Lord

I'm free

No longer bound

No more chains holding me

My soul is resting

It's such a blessing

Praise the Lord

Hallelujah

I'm free

Uplifting, mystical, and, yes, accepting of the inevitability of death in that eerie yet calming way we do in Black communities, it was these lyrics that sent me into a convulsion of sobs, the words so uncomplicated yet so loaded with meaning, pathos, and power. It dawned on me, then and there Shallon, that my aunt was now free to be the woman she did not get to be in life. Except now it would be in a different space, in a different world, one we cannot yet quite visualize, a space and a world where she could finally be happy—and whole. And as my aunt's casket was lowered into the ground at Richardson Cemetery, right next to St. John's AME Church, the talk almost instantaneously turned, amongst my other two aunts and mother, from Pearlie Mae to who would be next. A gloomy appreciation came over me that their concerns were so very real when considering the three remaining sisters: My Aunt Birdie has had multiple heart attacks; my mother has acute diabetes and a very bad leg that forces her to walk with a limp; and my Aunt Cathy had an emotional breakdown a year or so after my grandmother's death and wound up in both a mental institution and a welfare hotel for a spell. So there these women were, not only marking off the grave plots for themselves and my uncle, but also speaking, with both trepidation and a nonchalant sense of the inescapable, about the time when they will be free, no longer bound.

No longer bound, Shallon, by that very first biblical tale that put the world's problems, moral dilemmas, and faults squarely at the feet of Eve, the woman, while Adam, the man, got a pass. No longer bound by a world that said a girl, a young woman, a fully grown woman, could not aspire to anything higher than being a mother, a caretaker; she could be the boss's secretary, but never the boss herself. No longer bound by an education that whitewashed women from history, save Betsy Ross sewing a flag and Rosa

Parks refusing to give up her seat on that Montgomery bus. No longer bound by the steady bombardment of disparaging images, be it *Girls Gone Wild* or the latest semi-pornographic music video or the cover of this or that male-centered American magazine. No longer bound by the idea that young girls should be stripped, selling their bodies and souls for the perverse pleasure of us man-children in the promised land. No longer bound by a society that does not value the work of women and, thusly, does not give them equal pay for work equal to that of their male counterparts. No longer bound by political or religious zealots who feel it their divine right to tell a woman what she can and cannot do with her body. No longer bound by men who think it a measure of their manhood to manipulate, beat, molest, rape, or murder a woman or a girl simply because they can. And no longer bound by the out of date gender roles women and girls have been assigned to keep us men and boys firmly in command.

Shallon, my Aunt Pearlie Mae may never have been physically beaten, as Kewaii had been, but she was emotionally assaulted, spiritually castigated, and severely marginalized in some way or another, her entire life, because she was a woman. The self-liberation theme embedded in Ntozake Shange's play *For Colored Girls Who Have Considered Suicide When the Rainbow Is Enuf* never touched my aunt's life. Nor did my aunt know she could use her voice to sing songs of freedom as Nina Simone had. History and culture, when told solely from the perspective of us men, us boys, has an uncanny way of rendering women and girls invisible, devoid of meaning, stray branches without a root. So my Aunt Pearlie Mae did not know that women with "umble" lives like hers had done remarkable things, had become leaders of movements, of one nation or another. But when you are bound, as she was, as your friend Kewaii was, by the forces of an unnatural and unholy alliance between mankind and the follies of our power plays, why would you ever contemplate a universe where you, a woman, could have power, too?

And isn't this what it is all about, Shallon, power? In your letter to me you mentioned how Kewaii's husband tried to control everything about her—from the way she wore her hair to the way that she dressed and the people she talked to. And over time, he isolated her from her close friends (yourself included) and most of her family. Sadly, most of us males do not get that it is truly the highest form of powerlessness to use our gender, our physical strength, our mind games, to exert power and control over females. Real power, regardless of the gender of the person with power, is about spirituality, morality, love, and seeing some form of love

BE IT DOMESTIC VIOLENCE, EQUAL PAY, SEXUAL HARASSMENT IN THE WORKPLACE, OR THE EXCLUSION OF WOMEN FROM THE CORRIDORS OF LEADERSHIP, IT IS ALWAYS, AGAIN, ABOUT POWER.

in every human being we encounter. Real power is about sharing, not ruling and dictating. Kewaii's husband did not love her, Shallon. He never did, because he never loved himself. No one who claims to love someone, yet seeks to harm, hurt, or undermine that person in some way, can truly say he understands what love is. I am finally figuring it out, in my early forties, Shallon. But I am so glad I am no longer that man who hurt women in the past and so glad I did not bring children into the world when I was but a child in mindset myself. Think of the many millions of us who have, who believe it is our birthright to maim, terrorize, and murder because we ourselves are so deeply wounded and we do not even know who we are. Most men don't realize that we imprison ourselves when we behave in this fashion; it is ultimately as disempowering to us as it is to women, albeit differently.

This is the dilemma, the great challenge for these times. If we are serious about change, then what does that word mean in terms of how a nation, any nation, treats its female population. Be it domestic violence, unequal pay, sexual harassment in the workplace, or the exclusion of women from the corridors of leadership, it is always, again, about power. For example, Shallon, although I supported Barack Obama for president, I would be lying if I said that I did not feel very acutely the pain of those disappointed female Hillary Clinton supporters, women of all races and class backgrounds, who shared a faint hope that America would finally catch up to nations as different as England, India, Argentina, Israel, Dominica, Canada, New Zealand, Ukraine, Liberia, Pakistan, Iceland, Sri Lanka, Ireland, and Rwanda and finally dedicate itself to achieving women's political leadership in mass numbers. Yes, Rwanda has already eclipsed us in women's political leadership, and we in America certainly have not experienced anything remotely close to what Rwanda experienced in the 1990s, when genocide occurred on a mass scale. The slaughter of five hundred thousand to one million ethnic Tutsis and dissident Hutus by Hutu militias in 1994—many by their own neighbors acting on the orders of the Hutu nationalist government—left Rwanda with a population that was 60 percent female and 40 percent male. During the genocide many women were raped and others widowed. Apart from their own memories of murder and of rape, they collectively faced a future of poverty, disease, and displacement. With thousands more men jailed for war crimes or living as refugees in neighboring Congo, Rwanda's women, at first by default, took on roles in business and politics. All too often, it is not until war devastates the systems of male domination that women are given opportunities to lead. Although Rwandan women had long enjoyed a relatively higher social status than some in other African nations, they still had weak property rights, and female entrepreneurs were rare. Rwanda's first Parliament in 1994 contained seventy seats with eight held by women. In 2003 the new constitution included a quota policy assuring women at least 30 percent of posts in decision-making organs. By 2008 Rwanda's Parliament made history when its lower house elected a majority (56.3 percent) of women members.

What Rwanda has done, in spite of the loss of huge chunks of its population to violence, is nothing short of remarkable—and historic. Women are now not only the majority in Parliament, but also a sizable portion of the entrepreneurial class, even as the nation begins to recover its former male-female ratio. In contrast, as of 2009, in America, where like most of the world the population is roughly half female, only 92 of the 441 members of the House of Representatives are women, or 17 percent. In the United States Senate, of the one hundred senators, only seventeen are women. And when we look at chief executive officers of Fortune 500 companies, it is not much different. So we in America must do more. I firmly believe that a larger percentage of women in leadership positions, across the board, will mean, once and for all, an end to the assaults and murders of women like Kewaii and the instituting of social programs, initiatives, to be sure, that will help women like my Aunt Pearlie Mae to be no longer bound by the historical shackles of sexism. Women should be able to reach their full human potential without fear of harassment or landmines marking their every step. And we must be more conscious and question the roles we assign to females from the time they are children. I am not interested in pointing the finger at any one person nor any one institution, but I am certain that somewhere in Kewaii's journey she was told, either directly or indirectly, that women should be submissive to men, that females are inferior to males. And if, Shallon, we are in fact to honor Kewaii's memory, and the memory of my Aunt Pearlie Mae, we must be willing to tell our children the truth, we must teach them to love, and to love hard, to embrace nonviolence as the only option for any form of beef or disagreement. And we must teach them, both the boys and the girls alike, that it is not correct, nor human, for girls, for women, to be viewed and treated as second-class citizens, or sex objects, or punching bags, in our so-called civilization. What are the lessons here for Kewaii's twelve- and eleven-year-old girls, Shallon? What are we going to teach them, and all little girls growing up in America, about self-worth, about self-esteem, about self-love, if we

WE WOULD BE LYING TO OURSELVES, STILL, IF WE DIDN'T ADMIT THAT MRS. CLINTON WAS SCRUTINIZED IN A WAY NO MAN HAD EVER BEEN

choose to remain silent when someone says, without pause "all men are created equal" but never bothers to include women in those conversations about liberty and the pursuit of happiness? We can only ensure that Kewaii's daughters do not continue the cycle of abusive relationships and female disenfranchisement if we tell them, forthrightly, about the power that women have. That means even seemingly minute things, like the American media's fascination with Michelle Obama's wardrobe, should be challenged. It needs to be stated to girls across America, explicitly, that Michelle Obama is Barack Obama's equivalent on every single level, that he needs her as much as she needs him, that they are in a partnership, one rooted in love and respect for each other's lives, each other's leadership, each other's humanity. And Kewaii's nine-year-old boy must be told the truth of what his father did, not to shock or scare him, but to let him know that he should aspire to break the spinning wheel of violence that claimed his father's sanity and his mother's life. He should understand that his father did a very terrible thing, but that as the next generation, he is free to choose a different path. He need never put his hands on a female, verbally or mentally abuse a female, or feel that his major function in life is to control, dominate, and terrorize women or girls.

The steady hand of male authority in our society fuels violence against women and girls and prevents them from obtaining the cultural, economic, and political empowerment to end it. That is why Hillary Clinton, when she conceded the Democratic nomination to Barack Obama, referred to her bid for president of the United States as "that highest, hardest glass ceiling." We would be lying to ourselves, still, if we didn't admit that Mrs. Clinton was scrutinized in a way no man had ever been, including Barack Obama. There were juvenile references to her emotional disposition, to her temperament, to her style of dress (and rude questions about why she did not wear a dress more often), as if a woman could not lead a nation. I point, once more, to nations like Chile that have put such myths to rest by electing their first female head of state. But, for sure, Hillary Clinton did get eighteen million votes and did, as she put it, create "eighteen million cracks" in the glass ceiling. So something is stirring in America, Shallon, something really is. I heard someone say, once, that if the women move, then the entire nation will move. No, nothing can bring back the life of Kewaii Rogers-Buckner. Nor can anything bring back the life of my dear Aunt Pearlie Mae Powell. These women both lived the lives that they were handed, they meant no one any harm, and they both, I am sure, believed mightily in God, in some higher power, to sustain them. And they both, for very different reasons, died very sad, lonely, excruciatingly painful deaths. But what we must do, we who believe so firmly in the possibility of change and hope, is not allow their lives to be in vain. What we must do is first acknowledge that women have always been leaders, have always been powerful and, acknowledge, too, that it is not merely exceptions to the rule, as some would suggest, like Hillary Clinton or Michelle Obama, but the incalculable numbers of anonymous women, down through history, who have built and created, fought back, organized, and, yes, used their voices to resist the sexism and the various forms of violence in their lives.

Let us give names to these women: That woman is you, Shallon Patton, and Kewaii's mother, who organized a domestic violence candlelight vigil in Kewaii's honor. That woman is Myra Drake, relative to Lechea Wiggins Crawford and Lechea's sister and tiny children (all murdered by Lechea's husband in Cleveland), who has created a website to not only memorialize them, but to also serve as a learning tool for other victims of domestic violence. That woman is Lourdes Loradin, whose cousin Monica Paul was gunned down in front of a Montclair, New Jersey, YMCA. Lourdes is leading the charge to pass *Monica's Law* in her home state, a law that would put forth four specific changes to current laws around domestic violence, and help other women going forward. What is her name? That woman is my dear friend Erykah Franklin, who suffered through a marriage of emotional abuse, neglect, and little to no financial or moral backing, while raising two little sons, seemingly on her own. Erykah could have given up, could have broken down, and I would not have blamed her one bit. But she did not. Instead she survived a nasty divorce, charity from relatives and friends, many days and nights of trying to find money for food or gas, and obtained her PhD, against all odds, and is now a college professor at a major American university, in a state far away from the aches of her past life. That woman is Ai-jen Poo, lead organizer for Domestic Workers United, a coalition of Caribbean, Latina, Asian, and African housekeepers, nannies, and elderly caregivers in New York. These working-class women toil in some of my city's wealthiest neighborhoods, yet they have been isolated and excluded from almost every major labor law. Their mission: a Domestic Workers Bill of Rights. They use their collective voice to lobby lawmakers, to rally and march, to host training sessions and teach-ins, and to provide services ranging from legal advice to help with navigating language barriers. That woman is Farrah Fawcett who, despite her very personal battle with cancer, allowed us into her life by means of a sensitive and touching documentary and, as a result, gave millions of others battling cancer the strength and courage to march forward. That woman is Lynn Nottage, Pulitzer Prize–winning playwright, whose hypnotic dramatic piece *Ruined* is the story of the heartbreaking impact of war on women in the Democratic Republic of Congo. That woman is Laura Dawn, creative director of MoveOn.org, leader, activist, artist, filmmaker, true renaissance woman, and one of the most passionate and amazing human beings I have ever met. There is no social justice issue that Laura does not think about, no cause not important enough for her, and not too many who have the kind of passion for life, and for people, that she does. That woman is my mother, Shirley Powell, and that woman is my aunt Catherine Powell, both of whom were forced to raise boys, my cousin Anthony and me, by themselves, after our fathers shirked their responsibilities and moved on to God only knows where. If we had known that the commonly held belief was that two undereducated and poor single mothers could not possibly bring up two boys on welfare, food stamps, Medicaid, and government cheese within the confines of run-down apartment buildings run roughshod by rats, roaches, and the piss-stained smell of mayhem and madness, I doubt seriously, Shallon, I would be writing this letter to you this very moment. But those women, my mother and my aunt, are leaders, and leaders figure out a way out of no way, leaders make do with what they have, and leaders do not hear the naysayers, do not see the doubters, do not believe that the impossible is not possible. My mother and my aunt rejected wholesale the perpetually lame argument that single mothers cannot raise boys to be men. I realize today, in this adult form, how much I internalized the voices and the energies of my mother and my Aunt Cathy as a child. If I speak for anyone else in this letter, Shallon, it is them, or perhaps it is their voices speaking through me, saying, We are proof that it can be done . . .

It can be done, Shallon Patton, all of the miracles and changes you want to see, and all the miracles and changes I want to see, too. I do really believe that, and I have an everlasting hope that it will happen, in our lifetimes. We cannot bring Kewaii Rogers-Buckner or Pearlie Mae Powell back, for they are gone from us forever. But it is in our hands now, you, a woman, and I, a man, to turn this world on its heels and spin it in another direction—to place women and men on equal footing, at long last. Yes, and we must do something even greater than that. We must free ourselves to experience the kind of happiness and fulfillment that was denied Kewaii and Pearlie Mae from the very beginning. We will only be free when we know that the true measure of power and love lies in what we do during our lifetimes to place joy where there was hurt and sorrow, peace where there was trauma and conflict, dreams where there were nightmares, opportunity where there was despair, and life where there was death. When we can do that, Shallon, and do it consistently, for ourselves and for others, then we will be lifted up, as my Aunt Pearlie Mae's casket was elevated to the sky by that song of freedom. And we children of you women, we children of this Earth, will remix the words and chant, in unison, Praise the Lord, I am free, I am no longer bound, there are no chains holding me. And so it will be, Shallon. And so it will be—

Sincerely,

Kevin Powell

★ ★ ★ ACKNOWLEDGMENTS ★ ★ ★

So many to thank for making *Open Letters To America* possible: Richard Nash, Anne Horowitz, and all the wonderful folks associated with Soft Skull Press these past few years. Charlie Winton, Laura Mazer, Roxanna Aliaga, Abbye Simkowitz, Adam Krefman, Julie Pinkerton, Tiffany Lee and all the good people at Counterpoint. Kerry DeBruce, simply the best graphic designer on the planet. Joe Major, one of the best photographers around. My dear friends Marlo David, Rob Kenner, Lauren Summers, Lauren Teverbaugh, and Robyn Rodgers (a.k.a. DJ Reborn), all of who lent their incredible editorial eyes to various forms of this book. Lastly, I certainly want to thank all the people across America who inspired me to complete this essay collection.

★ *In The Tradition: An Anthology of Young Black Writers*
(1993; edited with Ras Baraka)

★ *recognize*
(1995; poetry by Kevin Powell)

★ *Keepin' It Real: Post-MTV Reflections On Race, Sex, and Politics*
(1997; essays by Kevin Powell)

★ *Step Into A World: A Global Anthology of The New Black Literature*
(2000; edited by Kevin Powell)

★ *Who Shot Ya? Three Decades of Hiphop Photography*
(2002; Photographs by Ernie Paniccioli/Edited by Kevin Powell)

★ *Who's Gonna Take The Weight? Manhood, Race, and Power in America*
(2003; essays by Kevin Powell)

★ *Someday We'll All Be Free*
(2006; essays by Kevin Powell)

★ *No Sleep Till Brooklyn*
(2008; poetry by Kevin Powell)

★ *The Black Male Handbook: A Blueprint for Life*
(2008; edited by Kevin Powell)